40 IS FINE IF YOU LOOK 29...

D1298362

By Herbert I. Kavet
Illustrated by Martin Riskin

Copyright © 1987

by Ivory Tower Publishing Company, Inc.

All Rights Reserved

No portion of this book may be reproduced - mechanically, electronically, or by any other means, including photocopying - without the permission of the publisher.

Published simultaneously in Canada by
Marka Canada, Toronto, Ontario

Manufactured in the United States of America

2 3 4 5 6 7 8 9 10 11 12 13 14 15 16 17 18 19 20 21 22 23 24 25 26 27 28 29 30

IVORY TOWER PUBLISHING COMPANY, INC.
125 Walnut Street, Watertown, MA 02172
TEL: (617) 923-1111   TELEX: 262992 ITAP

40 IS FINE IF YOU LOOK 29...

**And attractive women
still flirt with you.**

40 IS FINE IF YOU LOOK 29...

**And you're still one
of the best looking in your class.**

40 IS FINE IF YOU LOOK 29...

And you appreciate the quality engineering on a fine imported machine.

40 IS FINE IF YOU LOOK 29...

And keep your pets in their proper place.

40 IS FINE IF YOU LOOK 29...

And can't be intimidated
by the most complex computers.

40 IS FINE IF YOU LOOK 29...

**And you've finally paid back
your college loans.**

40 IS FINE IF YOU LOOK 29...

**And you still are
adventurous as ever with ethnic foods.**

40 IS FINE IF YOU LOOK **29**...

And have kids old enough to help.

40 IS FINE IF YOU LOOK 29...

And can hardly notice any hair loss.

40 IS FINE IF YOU LOOK 29...

**And can figure out
most anything that goes wrong with your car.**

40 IS FINE IF YOU LOOK 29...

And you realize how much good you did yourself when you stopped smoking.

40 IS FINE IF YOU LOOK 29...

**And you're smart enough
to hire kids to do the dog work
around your home.**

40 IS FINE IF YOU LOOK 29...

And you're into health foods.

40 IS FINE IF YOU LOOK 29...

**And can afford
to vacation at exotic foreign places.**

40 IS FINE IF YOU LOOK 29...

And women assume you think of them
as liberated equals.

40 IS FINE IF YOU LOOK 29...

**And you never get embarrassed
renting X-rated movies.**

40 IS FINE IF YOU LOOK 29...

**And your underwear
is as stylish as any in the locker room.**

40 IS FINE IF YOU LOOK 29...

**And you're still the same old tiger
on the road.**

40 IS FINE IF YOU LOOK 29...

And if you'd take the time
to lose 10 lbs. you'd be in better shape
than you were in high school.

40 IS FINE IF YOU DO 99...

And are smart enough
not to be talked into activities you can't handle.

40 IS FINE IF YOU LOOK 29...

**And you know
when you've had enough to drink.**

40 IS FINE IF YOU LOOK 29...

**And still can
look pretty good in a bathing suit.**

40 IS FINE IF YOU LOOK **29**...

**And can eat a hot fudge sundae
without worrying about breaking out.**

40 IS FINE IF YOU LOOK **29**...

And repair men can't bamboozle you anymore.

40 IS FINE IF YOU LOOK 29...

RAT TERDS
INTERNATIONAL
TOUR

**And you have stayed on top
of the latest music.**

40 IS FINE IF YOU LOOK 29...

**And you own
so much stuff no one knows what to buy you.**

40 IS FINE IF YOU LOOK 29...

And your memory is just as sharp as ever.

40 IS FINE IF YOU LOOK 29...

And they start to trust you at banks.

40 IS FINE IF YOU LOOK **29**...

**And your mother-in-law
finally starts to appreciate you.**

40 IS FINE IF YOU LOOK 29...

And teenagers are envious
of some of your adventures.

40 IS FINE IF YOU LOOK 29...

**And you're starting to be able
to afford things you don't really need.**

40 IS FINE IF YOU LOOK 29...

**And occupy a
position of responsibility at work.**

40 IS FINE IF YOU LOOK 29...

And can still remember
the punch lines to more than 4 jokes.

40 IS FINE IF YOU LOOK **29**...

And can still party with the best of them.

40 IS FINE IF YOU LOOK 29...

And you've recently assumed a mortgage that dwarfs the national debt.

40 IS FINE IF YOU LOOK 29...

**And you don't take any baloney
from wine stewards or haughty waitresses.**

40 IS FINE IF YOU LOOK 29...

And young people accept you as an equal.

40 IS FINE IF YOU LOOK 29...

And you truly know the value of a good friend.

40 IS FINE IF YOU LOOK 29...

And can still wear out most kids at your favorite sport.

40 IS FINE IF YOU LOOK 29...

And have a handle on all the latest fashions.

40 IS FINE IF YOU LOOK 29...

NUDE
BATHING
PERMITTED

And you can still fantasize
about going to a nude beach.

40 IS FINE IF YOU LOOK 29...

And start to make some real contributions in your field.

40 IS FINE IF YOU LOOK 29...

**And are smart enough
to pace yourself to finish sports events.**

40 IS FINE IF YOU LOOK 29...

**And feel secure
enough to dress for comfort.**

40 IS FINE IF YOU LOOK 29...

And can afford some really neat toys.

40 IS FINE IF YOU LOOK **29**...

And have a friend who recognizes your value enough to give you a book like this.

🐞 IVORY TOWER PUBLISHING COMPANY INCORPORATED 🐞

These other fun books are available at many fine stores or by sending $3.50 ea. directly to the publisher.

2000 - Do Diapers Give You Leprosy? A humorous look at what every parent should know about bringing up babies.

2008 - Adult Connect The Dots. You played connect the dots as a child, but never like this!

2015 - Games You Can Play With Your Pussy. And lots of other stuff cat owners should know.

2020 - A Coloring Book for Pregnant Mothers To Be. Tender and funny, from being unable to see the scale to controlling your proud parents.

2026 - Games You Can Play In Bed. A humorous compendium covering everything from Bedtime Bingo to Things To Do at 3:45 A.M.

2027 - How To Pick Up Girls. Bridget is back to show all philanderers some proper pick-up techniques.

2034 - You Know You're Over Forty When... You think "Grass" is something to cut and "Getting a little action" means your prune juice is working. A perfect 40th birthday gift.

2042 - Cucumbers Are Better Than Men Because... They don't care if you shave your legs, and they never walk around your place when the shades are up. At last, ladies, revenge for all our male chauvinist books.

2059 - Small Busted Women Have Big Hearts. Finally a book that boasts the benefits of being small busted in our society where bigger is better! A super way to bolster the ego of every slender woman.

2061 - I'd Rather Be 40 Than Pregnant... Or worrying about getting into graduate school, or travelling with young children, or getting no respect at a ritzy store. Great moral support for women reaching the diaperless age.

2064 - The Wedding Night - Facing Nuptial Terrors. For brides and grooms alike: What To Do If He Wants To Take Pictures; What To Do If She Won't Come Out Of The Bathroom; and many more hilariously funny situations newlyweds may encounter.

2065 - Best Mom In The World. The world's best Mom is the only one who can unclog toilets, sort everyone's socks and underwear, and bait fish hooks. A super gift for moms.

2066 - Dad, Best Friend In The World... Knows the value of a Sunday nap and knows enough not to give mom and the kids driving lessons. He is an expert explainer of the facts of life. A perfect gift for every father's day occasion.

2067 - It's Time To Retire When... Your boss is younger than you are, you stop to think and sometimes forget to start again, or you feel like the morning after and you swear you haven't been anywhere.

2068 - Sex Manual For People Over 30. Includes great excuses for non-performance, rediscovering foreplay, and how to tell an orgasm from a heart attack.

2101 - Peter Pecker's Guide To The Male Organ. A detailed analysis of the types of men who own Wee Wees, Members, Weenies, Dinks, Schlongs, No Nos, Tools, Wangs, and many others. Everyone is covered, from accountants to taxi drivers.

2102 - You Know You're Over 50 When... You add "God willing" to the end of most of your statements and you don't care where your wife goes when she goes out, as long as you don't have to go with her. A great 50 year old birthday gift.

2109 - The Get Well Book. Cheer up sick folks with this book that teaches them how to gain sympathy, what the doctor really means and how to cope with phones, kids, germs and critters that make you sick.

2121 - More Dirty Crosswords. This latest edition of dirty crosswords will test your analytical powers even further as you struggle to improve your vocabulary.

2123 - You Know You're Over 60 When... You're 60 when you start straddling two road lanes, you start looking forward to dull evenings at home, and you can't remember when prunes and figs weren't a regular part of your diet.

2126 - After All These Years. An Anniversary Book. Gives all the pluses and problems of marriage from learning to sleep without pillows or blanket to having someone around who can find all the really itchy spots on your back.

2127 - Your Golf Game Is In Big Trouble When... Your practice rounds are all in the bar and you've tried out 30 putters and none of them work and you play whole rounds without once hitting the fairway.

2129 - Fun In The John. More fun than you ever dreamed possible. Crosswords, Bathroom Lists, Word Searches, Mystery Games, John Horoscopes, Connect The Dots, Mazes, and Much More.

2130 - How To Tell If It Was Good. It was good if your partner can't stop repeating your name. It was bad if your partner can't remember your name. It was good if your partner wrote you poetry. It was bad if your partner wrote you a prescription.

2131 - The Fart Book. Farts are divided into two groups. 1. Your farts. 2. Somebody else's fart. This book lists them all, the Little Girls Don't Fart Fart, The Dog Did It Fart, the S'cuse me Fart and many more.

2136 - The Shit List - The list is quite extensive and describes the versatile use of this clever word. There is, for example, "chicken shit" and "give a shit" and "shoot the shit". A very funny book, noshit.

2142 - It's Nifty To Be 50. A new birthday book for women. It's Nifty to Be 50 when the kids are old enough to help willingly, and you can't be talked into activities you don't like in weather you hate.

2144 - Women Make Better Bosses Because... They understand when your child is sick, don't look down your dress and they'll hire cute guys for the office.

2149 - Working Mothers Don't Need Vacations and Other Myths. Of course, they have self-cleaning bathrooms, husbands who help and understanding bosses.

2152 - True Love Is... Keeping each other's secrets, sharing desserts and tolerating each other's pets.

2153 - Fart Part II. This sequel covers the dreaded "Thank God I'm Alone Fart", the insidious "SBD Fart" and the awe-inspiring "Sonic Boom Fart".

2156 - Pumping Tush. For all you exercise fanatics. Bridget explains locker room smells and gives suggestions for avoiding gasps in community showers.

2162 - The Booger Book. All boogers can be divided into two groups: 1) dry boogers; 2) wet boogers. This book covers them all, from the swimmer's booger to types of booger disposal techniques.

2165 - The Professional Homemaker Is... A Plumber, a Veterinary Assistant, a TV Analyst, a Domestic Management Specialist & many other things.

2166 - You've Survived Catholic School When... You can enter a phone booth without feeling you should begin confessing and you don't shudder when someone hands you a ruler.

2167 - The Official Chinese Sex Manual. An hour later you're horny again. Covers everything from petting below the pigtail to achieving orgasm with your chopsticks.

2168 - You Know You're A Year Older When... You no longer eat all the dessert just because it's there and you can no longer easily sleep till noon.

2169 - The Curse. Tasteful, sensitive, very funny and sympathetic. It's about a subject that plagues women each month.

2170 - If Your Birthday Falls On A Workday. Everything from how to get the day off to eating ice cream without a spoon.

2171 - Compliments To The Cook. "Great cooks never serve vegetables people can't spell" and "always have plausible excuses and sincere apologies ready."

2172 - The Perfect Lover. Turns into a pizza at 3 a.m., holds a Ph.D. in back rubbing & gets into bed first on cold nights just so you'll have warm sheets.

2173 - The Burp Book. Includes the difference between a burp and a belch; the skinny kid burp, the silent burp, the complimentary belch and many more.

2174 - Keep Fit With Drink. The Alcorobic way to build a better body. Walking the Line, the Sit-up, the Heave and more.

2175 - Asses. The complete directory of asses of all kinds from the Male Biker's Buns to the Oh Wow! Ass.

2176 - The First Time. From "how to tell if your date is thinking about sex" to "five great excuses for leaving in the middle of the night."

2177 - You're Over The Hill When... No one cares anymore about what you did in high school, and you see your old cereal bowl in an antique shop.

2178 - The Pregnant Father. The Pregnant Father's chief duty during delivery is to hold a little pan while his wife throws up into it...and much more!

2179 - Irish Sex Manual. Great Irish lovers share their favorite positions. Learn why Irish women are better and what Irish men love about sex.

2180 - Italian Sex Manual. Covers everything from picking up Italian men to great Italian sex games and why Italian men are better lovers.

2181 - Jewish Sex Manual. Includes detailed information about what Jewish women love about sex, how to pick up Jewish men and great Jewish blind dates.

2182 - Life Is Too Short To Date Ugly Men. Life is too short to forgo exotic vacations or never to cheat on your diet!

2183 - 50 Is Fine If You Look 39... And you can eat a hot fudge sundae without worrying about breaking out. Plus many more!

2184 - 60 Is Fine If You Look 39... And you can buy the car you want without worrying over whether it will hold ten kids, musical instruments and dogs. And more!

2186 - 40 Is Fine If You Look 29... And you're still the same old tiger on the road, and they start to trust you at banks and you can still party with the best of them. For MEN.

2187 - Big Busted Women Have More Fun... Big busted women somehow seem more motherly, get the most out of stretch fabric and always know where to look for a lost earring.

2188 - Great Sex For Busy Couples... Explains how to find the time, the place and the desire when two careers keep the couple running.

2189 - You're Aged To Perfection When... You stop worrying about your weight and you're smart enough to save out-of-style clothing until it becomes fashionable again.

2190 - Teddy Bears Are Better Than Men Because... They don't hog the whole bed and they invariably understand when you have a headache.

2191 - Your Skiing's Going Downhill When... Ski shops refuse to tune your skis and you start thinking about the hot tub before your first run.

IVORY TOWER PUBLISHING CO., INC.   125 Walnut Street, Watertown, MA 02172   **(617) 923-111**